7.15

From the marsh to the table...

CRANBERRIES
REVEALED

Photography & Concept by

Wayne R. Martin

Published by
Martin *Photo*Media, LLC
Plymouth, MN

Published by
Martin *Photo***Media**, LLC
Plymouth, MN 55442
www.martinphotomedia.com

Library of Congress Control Number: 2014916369
ISBN: 978-0-9908129-0-6

Printed and bound in China
First Edition

Design and layout by Paul Earney — St. Croix Creative, Inc.

ATTENTION

Corporations, schools, professional organizations and trade groups:

Quantity discounts are available on bulk purchases of this book for educational and gift purposes.

For information, contact **Martin** *Photo***Media** at (763) 551-0395 or wayne@martinphotomedia.com.

DEDICATION

My mother, **Mildred Martin**, worked tirelessly to help support our family as I was growing up. One of her many part-time seasonal jobs was working the cranberry harvest in the fall. Along with many other women from the Wisconsin Rapids area, she sorted berries on the processing line. (See page 62 for an example of that type of work.) Although modern processing methods have automated or eliminated many of the manual tasks, you can still see women sorting cranberries today—just as my mom did. So I salute all hardworking cranberry sorters, past, present, and future—but especially my mom!

FOREWORD

Native Americans have harvested and eaten wild cranberries since long before the arrival of European settlers. After the first Thanksgiving at Plymouth Colony in 1621, the succulent cranberry became synonymous with holiday dinners across America.

Cranberry cultivation has been an important agricultural endeavor in Wisconsin since the mid-nineteenth century. Today, more than half of all cranberries harvested in the United States are grown there. They are also an important fruit crop in Massachusetts, New Jersey, Oregon, Washington, and the Canadian provinces of British Columbia and Quebec.

Cranberries are one of three indigenous fruits unique to North America that are commercially cultivated. Prized for their antioxidant nutritional properties, the tart berries lend their unique flavor to baked goods, juices, and sauces. Sweetened dried berries have become a popular snack and recipe ingredient. Nearly a thousand food and beverage products contain cranberries, making them more than just a holiday staple.

Photographer Wayne Martin grew up in the cranberry country of Central Wisconsin. Since childhood he has been fascinated by the environment around him. His first experience with cranberries was sampling lip-puckering, highly concentrated cranberry juice served at a local bank—a tart tasting experience he never forgot.

PART ONE

ART AND BEAUTY
OF THE CRANBERRY

A CLOSER LOOK

When immersed in water and frozen, cranberries take on an otherworldly appearance.

The four chambers
of the fruit make it
very buoyant—an
advantageous
property at
harvest time.

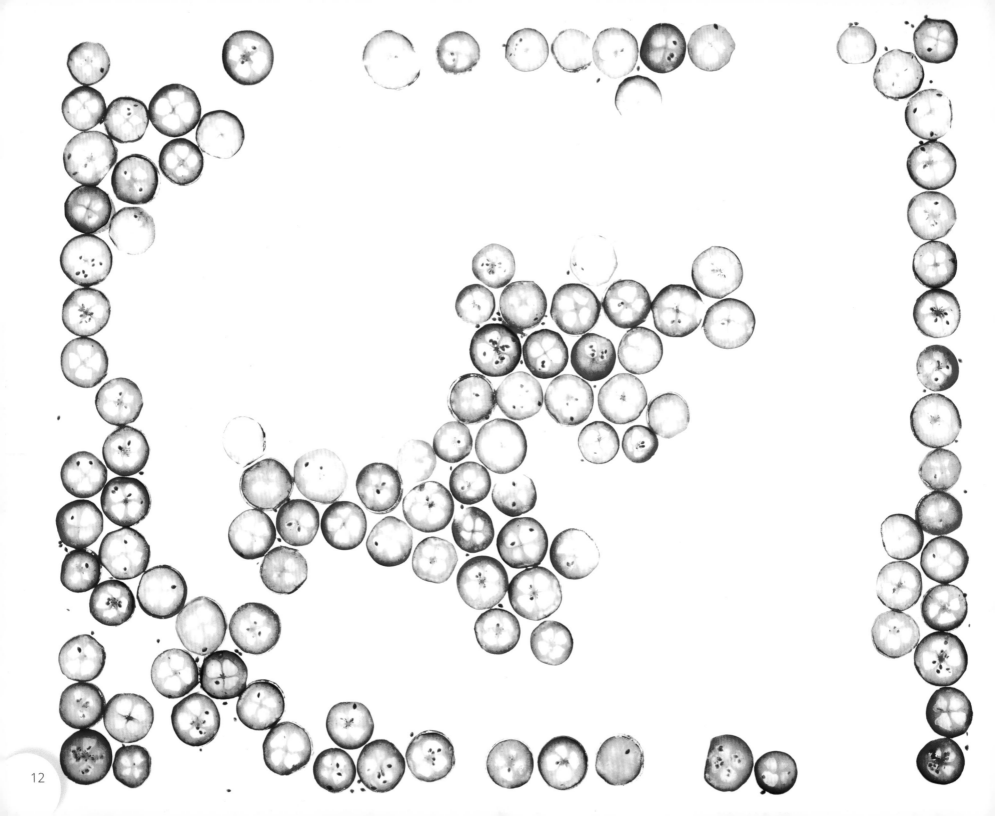

The cranberry's tiny seeds, its genesis,
emerge inside the chambers.

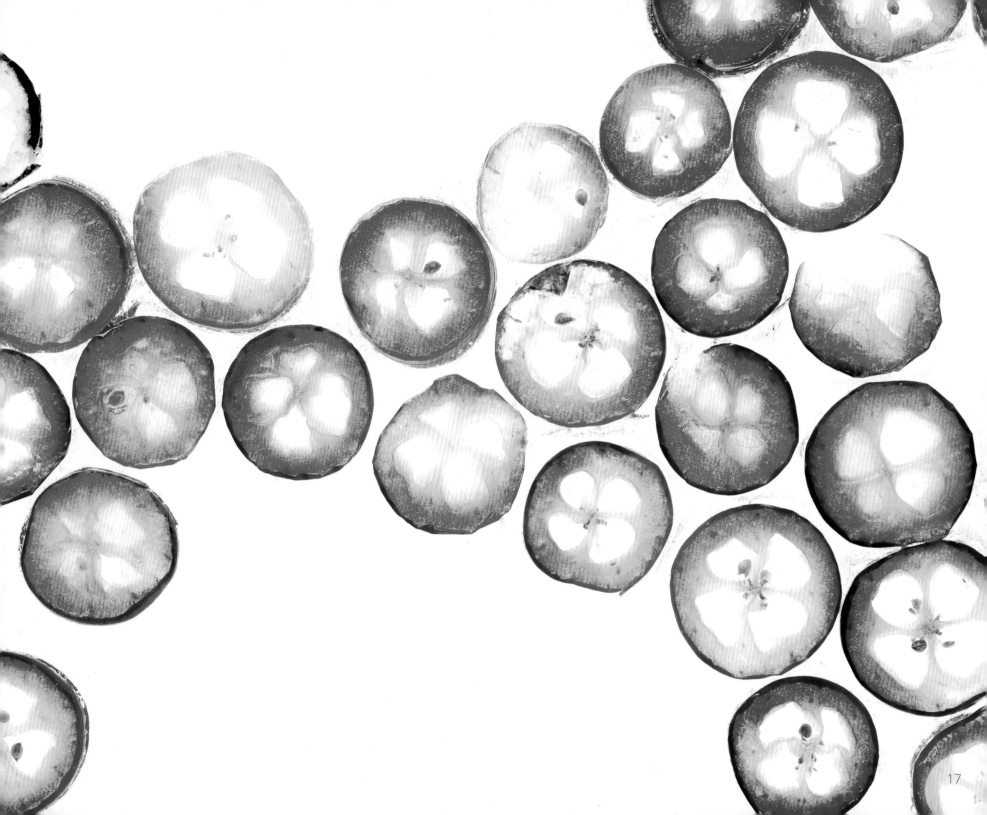

PART TWO

CRANBERRY

THE MARSH

In late September, when
the water exceeds that of
fog rises from the marsh
sun intensifies the effect

"Crane berry" was what early settlers called the plant whose blossoms resembled the bill of the sandhill crane.

Wildlife abounds in the wetlands of cranberry country.
Sandhill cranes, Canadian geese, eagles, otters, muskrat, wild turkeys, and deer frequent the marshes.

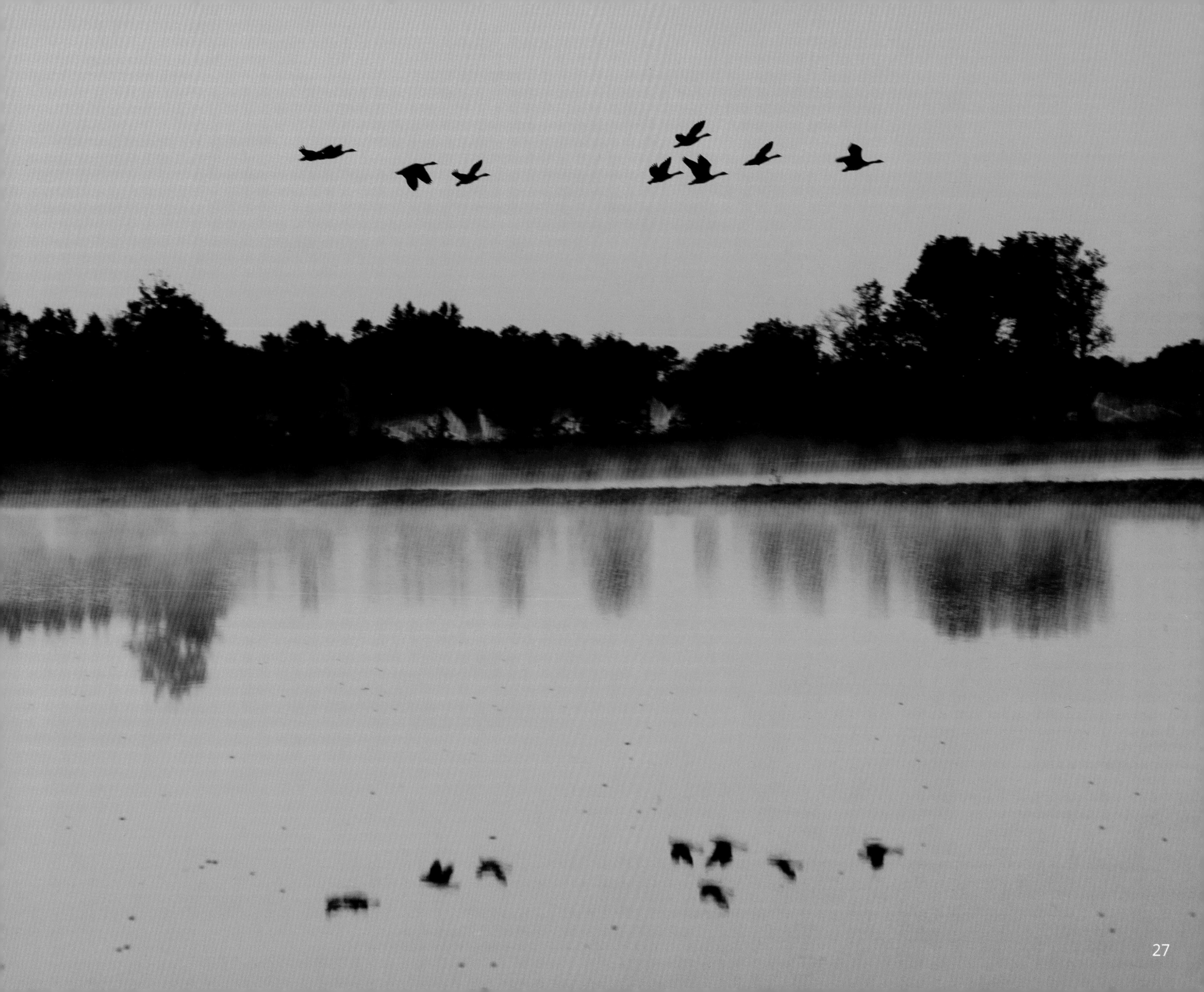

A bald eagle scans the flooded landscape in search of its next meal.

White swans glide through a submerged bed, oblivious to the harvest activity around them.

Autumn's cool days and frosty nights signal the approaching cranberry harvest.

CRANBERRY CULTURE

THE HARVEST

Brian Ruesch grows organic cranberries. Here, he harvests them by hand in the traditional manner, using a cranberry rake.

Yes, there are wild cranberries. But they are rare.
Brian Ruesch reveals these seldom-seen beauties
at his Century Farm in Vesper, Wisconsin.

A powerful, red-filtered light used during a thirty-second exposure reveals berries just after sunset at Gaynor Cranberry Company.

Why do cranberry growers use irrigation sprinklers on their crop in the fall? For the same reason citrus growers do: to protect the crop from damaging frosts. Viewed from above, the sprinklers' spray forms ever-moving patterns.

It is commonly thought that cranberries grow underwater. That is not true. Flooding the beds prevents the plants from freezing and makes the berries easier to harvest.

Trucks line up on a dike at sunrise, waiting to transport berries once they are harvested.

A network of earthen dikes separates the cranberry beds and allows growers to control the water levels in each.
They also serve as access roads for the machinery used to plant, fertilize, and harvest the fruit.

Two traditional mainstays of Central Wisconsin's economy, paper mills *(background)* and cranberry marshes *(foreground)*, use water drawn from the adjacent Wisconsin River near Biron, Wisconsin.

A common way to harvest cranberries is beating them off the vine with mechanized rotating reels or tines. They then float to the surface of the water, where they are easy to gather. Berries harvested in this manner are sold in the processed fruit market—that is, they are used for juices, sweetened dried berries, and sauces. Only 5 percent of the harvest is sold as fresh fruit.

Autumn's splendor of color surrounds
this harvest operation near Wisconsin Rapids.

Against a backdrop of fall colors, workers move a containment boom into position at the end of a cranberry bed.

A worker secures a connector on the containment boom.

Berries that have been beaten off the vine are corralled inside the containment boom, which concentrates them into a smaller area from which they can be conveyed onto trucks.

This bird's-eye view shows how berries are collected and then conveyed onto a truck at Gaynor Cranberry Company in Cranmoor, Wisconsin.

Surrounded by a sea of red, workers coax the berries toward a partially submerged conveyor that loads the fruit onto a truck.

Berries cascade into a truck at Glacial Lake Cranberries in Cranmoor, Wisconsin. They will later be transported to an on-site facility for processing.

A worker removes an irrigation head, allowing the harvester to continue forward.

Empty "boats" float along the edge of a bed, waiting to be coupled to an ATV that will follow a mechanical harvester.

Habelman Brothers Company, the world's largest grower of fresh cranberries, uses mechanical rakers to harvest their berries. Raking provides a gentler touch that allows the berries to be sold as fresh fruit.

Workers shovel berries away from the edge of the bed and into the path of a harvester. Very few are missed.

Berries are dumped into trucks and then transported to a warehouse for processing.

The Warrens Cranberry Festival in Warrens, Wisconsin, celebrates the fall harvest.
Held on the last weekend of September, it attracts nearly 150,000 visitors.

CRANBERRY CULTURE

THE PROCESSING

Berries pass over a blower/dryer that
rids them of unwanted vines and
excess moisture at Habelman Brothers
Company in Tomah, Wisconsin.

Cleaned berries are loaded into wooden boxes and put into cold storage.

"Good" berries are separated from "bad" berries using a time-tested bouncing sorter called a Bailey Mill.

Because "bad" berries don't bounce, they are easily separated from the good ones that do—a simple, low-tech idea that is still widely used.

Berries that pass the bounce test are sent on their way to be packaged.

Automated optical sorting machines make quality control extremely fast and efficient. Yet the berries still must pass the most critical inspection tool of all: the human eye.

Sorted and inspected, berries are then bagged, boxed, and shipped to markets all over the world.

PART THREE

CRANBERRY INSPIRATIONS

THE RECIPES

They're not just for Thanksgiving anymore!

Because cranberries are a fruit, cooks commonly assume that they are best served as a dessert or beverage. However, cranberries complement dishes in every course, as the following recipes demonstrate.

The Wisconsin State Cranberry Growers Association, Warrens Cranberry Festival, and several individuals provided these recipes. Many of the WSCGA recipes were 2009 and 2010 Wisconsin State Fair award winners. The Warrens Cranberry Festival recipes were recent contest winners or top finishers.

64

CRANBERRY ORANGE OATMEAL COOKIES

by **Barbara A. Driscoll**

2010 Wisconsin State Fair Winner

2 sticks unsalted butter, softened
3/4 cup granulated sugar
1/4 teaspoon salt
2 egg yolks
1 teaspoon vanilla
2 1/2 cups all-purpose flour

1 cup sweetened dried cranberries
3/4 cup old-fashioned rolled oats
2 teaspoons freshly grated orange zest
About 1/2 cup sugar

In a large bowl beat together butter, sugar, and salt until light and fluffy. Beat in yolks one at a time. Add vanilla and beat until smooth. Beat in flour gradually, beating until just combined.

In a bowl soak cranberries in warm water to cover 15 minutes. Drain well and chop fine. Preheat oven to 350 degrees. Beat cranberries, oats, and zest into cookie dough. Form dough into 1-inch balls and roll balls in sugar to coat. Arrange balls 2 inches apart on baking sheets and flatten to 2-inch rounds with bottom of a glass wrapped in wax paper to prevent sticking.

Bake about 12 minutes until golden brown.

CRANBERRY BAKED CHICKEN

provided by the **Wisconsin State Cranberry Growers Association**

4 boneless, skinless chicken breast halves
  (around 1 1/2 pounds)
3/4 cup fresh or frozen cranberries
1/4 cup sugar
1 small chopped onion
1/2 teaspoon grated orange peel
1/2 cup orange juice
1/8 teaspoon ground cinnamon
1/8 teaspoon ground ginger

Combine all ingredients except chicken in a saucepan and bring to a boil. Put chicken in an ovenproof dish and pour sauce on top.

Bake uncovered at 375 degrees for 1 hour or more, until chicken is done.

CRANBERRY WILD RICE PILAF

provided by the **Wisconsin State Cranberry Growers Association**

3/4 cup uncooked wild rice
3 cups chicken broth
1/2 cup pearl barley
1/4 cup dried cranberries
1/4 cup dried currants
1 tablespoon butter or margarine
1/3 cup sliced almonds, toasted

Rinse and drain rice; place in a saucepan. Add broth and bring to a boil. Reduce heat; cover and simmer for 10 minutes. Remove from heat; stir in barley, cranberries, currants, and butter. Spoon into a greased 1 1/2-quart baking dish.

Cover and bake at 325 degrees for 55 minutes or until liquid is absorbed and rice is tender. Add almonds and fluff with a fork.

Makes 6–8 servings.

CRANBERRY CAKE WITH CARAMEL SAUCE

provided by my mother, **Mildred Martin**

1 cup granulated sugar
3 tablespoons melted butter
1 egg, beaten
1 cup milk
2 cups all-purpose flour
2 teaspoons baking powder
1/2 teaspoon salt
2 cups whole cranberries, washed

Cake:
Preheat oven to 350 degrees. Grease 9x13-inch pan. Cream butter, sugar, and egg. Add milk and mix. Blend flour, salt, and baking powder. Add to creamed mixture and mix well. Fold in whole drained cranberries. Bake 30 to 40 minutes. Allow to cool.

Caramel Sauce:
1 cup packed brown sugar
1 cup granulated sugar
3 tablespoons butter
1 cup milk

Heat sugars, butter, and milk in saucepan over medium-high heat for 5 minutes. Stir often until sugars are dissolved. Cool to warm. Slice cooled cake and ladle warm sauce over slices.

CRANBERRY PISTACHIO SAUCE

provided by the **Wisconsin State Cranberry Growers Association**

1 pound (4 cups) fresh or frozen cranberries
1 cup sugar
1 jar (10 oz) red currant jelly
1 cup orange juice
1/2 cup chopped pistachio nuts

Mix cranberries, sugar, jelly, and orange juice in 2-quart saucepan. Heat to boiling; reduce heat. Simmer uncovered 20 minutes, skimming off any foam that collects on surface. Remove from heat. Stir in nuts.

Appetizer Idea:
Top cream cheese with chilled Cranberry Pistachio Sauce, sprinkle with chopped pistachio nuts, and serve with crackers.

Keep leftover sauce in refrigerator.

It is a delicious accent to broiled salmon.
(See recipe on page 70.)

SALMON WITH CRANBERRY PISTACHIO SAUCE

provided by the **Wisconsin State Cranberry Growers Association**

2 pounds salmon fillet
2 tablespoons fresh lime juice
2 tablespoons butter or margarine, melted
1/2 teaspoon salt
chopped pistachio nuts, if desired
Cranberry Pistachio Sauce (see page 68)

Make Cranberry Pistachio Sauce; keep warm. Set oven control to broil. Spray broiler pan rack with cooking spray. Place fish, skin side down, on rack in broiler pan. Mix lime juice, butter, and salt; pour over fish.

Broil 4 inches from heat 8 to 10 minutes or until fish flakes easily with fork. Top fish with sauce. Sprinkle with nuts.

Makes 8 servings.

CRIMSON SLAW

2009 Wisconsin State Fair Winner

1/2 head red cabbage, shredded
1/2 red onion, thinly sliced
6 tablespoons olive oil
2 tablespoons red wine vinegar
2 teaspoons red wine
2 tablespoons sugar
1 teaspoon salt
1/2 teaspoon black pepper
1/4 teaspoon ground mustard
1 package (6 oz) sweetened dried cranberries

Mix cabbage and onion in large mixing bowl. In a second bowl, combine all other ingredients except cranberries and mix thoroughly. Pour over cabbage mixture, add the dried cranberries, and mix thoroughly. Marinate in refrigerator for at least one hour before serving.

FRUIT-STUFFED ACORN SQUASH

by Peggy West

2 medium acorn squash
1/4 teaspoon salt
2 cups tart apples, chopped and peeled
3/4 cup fresh or frozen cranberries
1/4 cup packed brown sugar
2 tablespoons butter or margarine, melted
1/4 teaspoon ground cinnamon
1/8 teaspoon ground nutmeg

Cut squash in half; discard seeds. Place squash cut side down in ungreased 9x13-inch baking dish. Add 1 inch of hot water to pan. Bake uncovered at 350 degrees for 30 minutes. Drain water from pan; turn squash cut side up. Sprinkle with salt. Combine the remaining ingredients; spoon into squash.

Bake 40 to 50 minutes longer or until squash is tender.

Makes 4 servings.

CRAZY GOOD COOKIES

by **Julie Robarge**
2010 Warrens Cranberry Festival Winner

1 cup butter
3/4 cup granulated sugar
3/4 cup packed brown sugar
2 eggs
1 teaspoon vanilla extract
3 cups quick-cooking oats
1 1/2 cups all-purpose flour
1 package (3.4 oz) instant vanilla pudding
1 teaspoon salt
1 teaspoon baking soda
1 cup chocolate chips
1 cup dried cranberries
1 cup chopped cashews

Preheat oven to 375 degrees. In a large mixing bowl, cream butter and sugars together; beat in eggs and vanilla. In separate bowl combine oats, flour, dry pudding mix, salt, and baking soda. Gradually add to wet mixture. Stir in chocolate chips, dried cranberries, and cashews. Drop by rounded teaspoons, 2 inches apart, onto ungreased cookie sheets.

Bake at 375 degrees for 10 to 12 minutes or until lightly browned. Move to wire racks and cool.

Makes approximately 4 dozen cookies.

SPICY CRANBERRY TURKEY WRAP

provided by the **Wisconsin State Cranberry Growers Association**

1 cup orange juice
1 cup sugar
1 bag (12 oz) cranberries, fresh or frozen*
1/2 cup currants or raisins
1/2 cup onion, diced
1/4 cup red wine vinegar
1 tablespoon jalapeño pepper, seeded and diced
1 teaspoon garlic, fresh or jarred, minced
3/4 teaspoon ground cumin
1 pound turkey breast cutlets
1/2 cup spreadable goat cheese or cream cheese
4 low-fat flour tortillas, 10-inch
4 large lettuce leaves, Romaine or leaf
1 tablespoon fresh cilantro, chopped
1 apple, thinly sliced

To make spicy cranberry sauce, place the first 10 ingredients in a medium saucepan. Boil 15 minutes, stirring occasionally, until cranberries burst and sauce thickens; refrigerate.

Sauté cutlets in lightly oiled skillet over medium heat, 5 minutes per side, until turkey is no longer pink in center and reaches internal temperature of 170 degrees. Cool and cut into strips. Spread 2 tablespoons of cheese over each tortilla to within 1/2 inch of edge. Layer lettuce, 1/2 cup turkey, 1/4 cup cranberry sauce, 1/2 teaspoon cilantro, and several apple slices on tortilla. Add salt and pepper to taste. Fold tortilla bottom and top over filling. Fold one side to center. Fold last side to overlap center and roll tight.

Makes 4 servings.

*For dried cranberries, soak with currants in orange juice for 8 hours.

DOUBLE CHOCOLATE CRANBERRY MUFFINS

by **Dawn Zastrow**
2009 Wisconsin State Fair Winner

Dry Ingredients:
1 3/4 cups all-purpose flour
3/4 cup granulated sugar
6 tablespoons unsweetened cocoa
2 1/2 teaspoons baking powder
3/4 teaspoon salt
1/2 cup semi-sweet chocolate or vanilla chips
2/3 cup fresh or frozen cranberries, chopped

Wet Ingredients:
2 eggs, beaten
3/4 cup milk
1/3 cup butter, melted

Topping:
1/2 cup semi-sweet chocolate chips
1 tablespoon shortening

Preheat oven to 400 degrees. Prepare 12-cup muffin pan by lightly greasing bottoms only. Stir first 5 dry ingredients together in large bowl. Stir in chips and cranberries. Beat wet ingredients together in mixer. Make a well in dry ingredients and pour wet ingredients into well. Stir just until moistened. Spoon batter about 2/3 full in each muffin cup.

Bake for 20 to 25 minutes or until done. Immediately turn out onto cooling racks.

Topping: Melt chocolate chips and shortening in microwave. Stir and drizzle over tops of muffins.

Makes 12 muffins.

Almond-Cranberry Bread with White Chocolate Glaze

by **Susan Nekich**
2009 Wisconsin State Fair Winner

Bread:
2 1/2 cups all-purpose flour
1 cup granulated sugar
3 teaspoons baking powder
1/2 teaspoon salt
1 cup buttermilk
1/4 cup butter, melted
2 eggs
1 1/2 cups frozen cranberries
2/3 cup sliced almonds, chopped
1 1/2 teaspoons almond extract

Glaze:
1/4 cup white chocolate chips
3 tablespoons powdered sugar
1–2 tablespoons milk OR 1–2 French Vanilla coffee creamers

Bread: In large bowl, mix flour, sugar, baking powder, and salt; set aside. Beat buttermilk, butter, eggs, and almond extract until blended. Stir in cranberries and nuts just until moist. Pour into greased and wax paper–lined 9x5-inch loaf pan. Bake at 325 degrees for 40 to 50 minutes, or until toothpick inserted comes out clean. Cool in pan on wire rack 10 minutes. Remove from pan. Cool completely.

Glaze: In microwave-safe bowl, microwave chips on high 30 seconds. Stir until melted. Beat in powdered sugar and thin with milk or coffee creamers to desired thickness. Drizzle icing over cooled loaf.

Optional: top with toasted almonds.

CRANBERRY WALNUT SWEET POTATOES

provided by the **Wisconsin State Cranberry Growers Association**

4 large sweet potatoes
1/4 cup onion, finely chopped
1 tablespoon butter
1 cup fresh or frozen cranberries
1/3 cup maple syrup
1/4 cup water
1/4 cup cranberry juice
1/4 teaspoon salt, divided
1/2 cup chopped walnuts, toasted
1 teaspoon Dijon mustard
1/4 teaspoon pepper
2 tablespoons minced chives

Scrub and pierce sweet potatoes. Bake at 400 degrees for 1 hour or until tender.

In a small saucepan, sauté onion in butter until tender. Add the cranberries, syrup, water, cranberry juice, and 1/8 teaspoon salt. Bring to a boil. Reduce heat; cover and simmer for 10 to 15 minutes or until berries pop, stirring occasionally. Stir in walnuts and mustard; heat through. Cut potatoes in half lengthwise; sprinkle with pepper and remaining salt. Top each with 2 tablespoons cranberry mixture; sprinkle with chives.

Makes 8 servings.

CRANBERRY SALAD

by **Cindy Winnemuller**
2009 Wisconsin State Fair Winner

3 cups (12 oz) fresh or frozen cranberries, chopped
1 can (20 oz) pineapple tidbits, drained
2 medium Granny Smith apples, peeled and chunked
1 cup green grapes
1 cup red grapes
2 cups miniature marshmallows
2/3 cup sugar
2 cups chopped walnuts
2 cups whipping cream, whipped

In a bowl, combine cranberries, pineapple, apple, grapes, marshmallows, sugar, and walnuts; mix well. Cover and refrigerate overnight. Just before serving, fold in whipped cream.

CRANBERRY SQUARES

by **Heather Cammack**

Dough:
1/2 cup butter
1 cup flour
5 tablespoons sugar

Filling:
2 eggs
1 1/2 cups sugar
1/4 cup flour
2 cups fresh cranberries, chopped

Mix dough ingredients. Spread on cookie sheet and bake for 10 minutes at 350 degrees.

Mix filling ingredients. (Cranberries can be chopped in food processor and remaining filling ingredients added.) Spread filling over the dough and bake for 35 minutes or until golden brown. Sprinkle with powdered sugar and cut into bars while hot, or they will be difficult to remove.

Makes about 3 dozen bars. Doubled, the recipe fills a large jelly roll pan and yields 5–6 dozen bars.

Birth of the Book

The images featured in part one were shot in a studio with photographic lighting in December 2009. The cranberries were photographed first as fresh fruit and then placed in a tray of water and frozen. The resulting slab of ice and fruit became the photographic subject. Although not an original idea, this concept has probably not been applied to cranberries before.

This visual exploration of the cranberry outside its natural environment was intriguing. When frozen, the berries formed remarkable frosty textures and random compositions. That led to photographing cranberries in their marshland environment and documenting the harvest and processing of the fruit. Viewing the marshes during the early hours of the morning and fading light of the day provided unexpected encounters with a wide variety of wildlife, as well as stunning images of the plants and berries.

What started out as a photographic experiment with frozen cranberries evolved into a surprising photographic journey—one filled with the spectacular beauty of cranberries and the marshlands where they grow.

Acknowledgments

Without the help of friends, family, the cranberry growers, and others, this book would never have been published. A huge debt of gratitude goes to my loyal friend **Tom Enwright**. Because of his previous employment in the cranberry industry, he was a compendium of knowledge connecting me to the right people. No Tom, no book—it's that simple.

It began on a cold day in February 2010 when Tom arranged a meeting with **Jerry Bach** and **John Stauner** in Wisconsin Rapids to explore the idea of doing this book. A lucky encounter with **Phil Brown** and **Mary Brazeau Brown** of Glacial Lake Cranberries a few weeks later led to an invitation to shoot their harvest in the fall of 2010.

Thanks to **Bob Wilson** at The Cranberry Network for connecting me to **Ray Habelman Jr. and his wife, Staci**, of Habelman Brothers Company in Tomah, Wisconsin, who allowed me to photograph their fresh harvest cranberry operation.

The Wisconsin State Cranberry Growers Association is the definitive source of all things cranberry in Wisconsin. Former WSCGA assistant Jane Anderson graciously passed along the Wisconsin State Fair recipe winners. **Kim Schroeder**, general manager of the Warrens Cranberry Festival, did the same with their Cranfest recipe winners. Thanks go to **Heidi Slinkman** of Gaynor Cranberry Company for allowing me to photograph her marsh during the WSCGA-sponsored media day, and to **Kris Naidl** of Zeppos & Associates for allowing me access to their helicopter during that event. A no-frills, early morning flight with **John Todd** in his ultra-light revealed stunning aerial panoramas, well worth the "agony of de feet" caused by whatever the wind chill was at 32 degrees with a 45 mph airspeed.

Brian Ruesch of Ruesch Century Farm provided a unique perspective on the art of growing organic berries and a surprising look at some wild cranberries. His berries are the "hero" berries of all my recipe shots.

My great friends and mentors, **Lee and Jean Kanten**, whose own creative abilities could have produced this book, supplied helpful ideas, creative writing, and editing assistance and support for which I am forever grateful. The helpful suggestions of **Bruce Nimmer**, food photographer extraordinaire, enabled me to take some baby steps into his world of expertise.

Many thanks to **Kellie Hultgren** of KMH Editing for picking all the nits that I didn't even know were there. Her laser-focused eye for details is uncanny.

My longtime friend and graphic designer, **Paul Earney**, is responsible for this book's beautiful design and layout. His creative presentation of my photographs has always made them look their best, and I am grateful to him in so many ways for bringing this book to life.

And last, but not least, thanks to **my wife, Anne, and daughters, Kelly and Katie**, for their support, honest critique, and patience as I roam far and away to get my images. You've put up with my photographic obsession forever. Thanks for your patience and understanding.

REVEALED!